THE
Fantastic
CUTAWAY BOOK OF
SPEED

JON RICHARDS *AND* ALEX PANG

ALADDIN/WATTS
LONDON • SYDNEY

CONTENTS

This edition published
in 2004
© Aladdin Books Ltd
1997

All rights reserved

Created by David West
and Alex Pang for
Aladdin Books Ltd
28 Percy Street
London W1T 2BZ

First published in Great
Britain in 1997 by
Aladdin/Watts
96 Leonard Street
London EC2A 4XD

ISBN 0 7496 5473 2

A catalogue record for
this book is available
from the British Library.

Printed in UAE

Editor
Simon Beecroft
Consultant
Steve Allman

Design

David West
CHILDREN'S BOOK DESIGN
Designer
Robert Perry

Picture research
Brooks Krikler Research

Illustrators Alex Pang
and Graham White

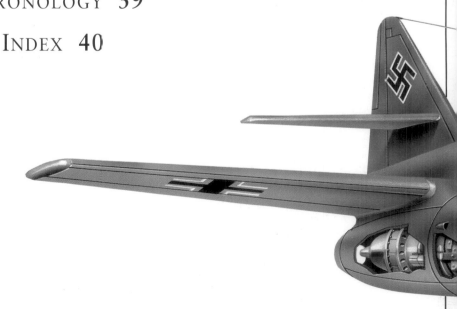

INTRODUCTION

Since the earliest days of powered transport, people have always felt the desire to make their cars, boats and planes go faster. In this quest for speed, designers and builders have continuously battled against the restricting forces of nature and physics. The drivers and pilots themselves have risked their lives – and often lost them – driving cars, steering boats or flying planes. The search to find ways of pushing the performance of vehicles beyond the existing limits never ceases.

The result has been the development of some amazing machines, all capable of reaching breath-taking speeds. These range from boats, that can lift themselves out of water and literally fly across the surface, to cars powered by enormous jet and rocket engines, and planes that can reach the edge of the Earth's atmosphere.

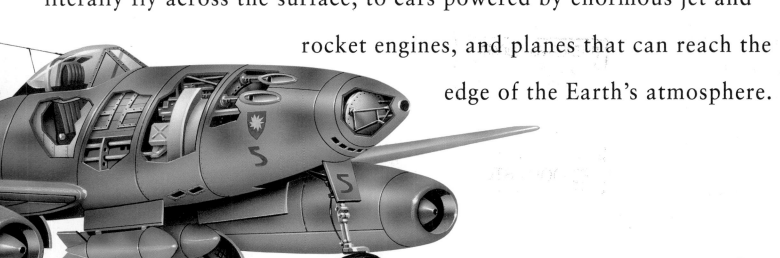

THE MCLAREN F1 is one of the most outstanding supercars ever built. It was designed using the technical skills of the McLaren motor racing team. Since its launch in 1992, the racing version, the F1 GTR (below), has gone on to win the 24-hour endurance race at Le Mans and the Global Endurance GT Series. The road-going version, the F1 LM (main picture), is no less thrilling to drive. It has a top speed of 360 km/h (225 mph) – making it one of the fastest cars on the road. It is able to accelerate from a standing start to 96 km/h (60 mph) in under three seconds, and it can reach 160 km/h (100 mph) in a little under five seconds!

McLaren F1 GTR

McLaren F1 LM

KEEPING LIGHT

The weight of the F1 LM is kept down to only 1,062 kg (2,336 lb) by the use of strong but light-weight materials, such as aluminium and carbon fibre, in the car's construction. By combining a lightweight car with a powerful engine, the designers were able to ensure that the F1 could accelerate at a phenomenal rate.

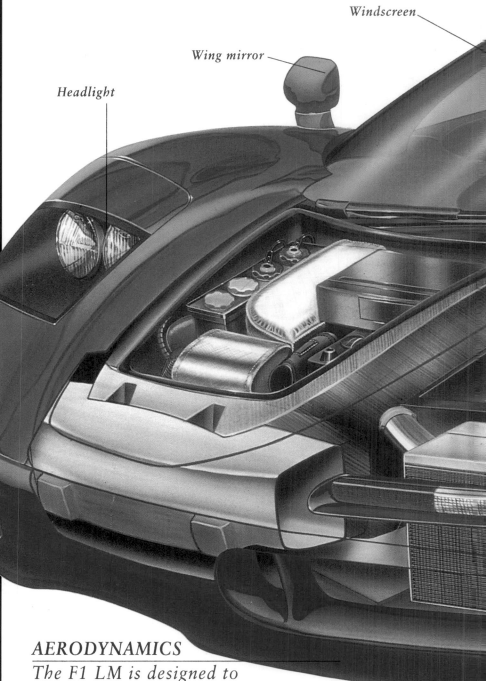

Windscreen

Wing mirror

Headlight

AERODYNAMICS

The F1 LM is designed to slice through the air and yet stick to the road. Road-holding is aided by large fans on the bottom of the car. These suck air from underneath, increasing the downforce on the car. This, in effect, glues the car to the road, allowing it to take bends and corners with greater speed.

BMW MOTORSPORT ENGINE

ENGINE POWER
The F1 is powered by a 6.1-litre (372-cubic inch) V-12 BMW engine (left). At 7,800 revolutions per minute (rpm) it can deliver an amazing 668 brake horsepower (bhp).

THE McLAREN F-1

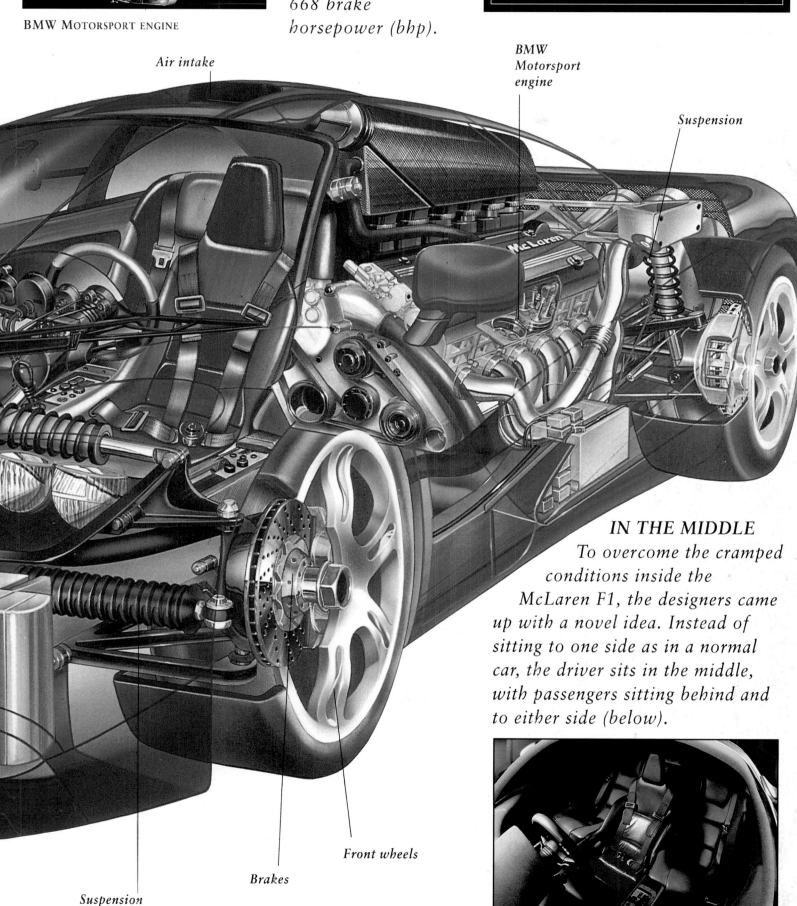

Air intake

BMW Motorsport engine

Suspension

Suspension

Brakes

Front wheels

IN THE MIDDLE
To overcome the cramped conditions inside the McLaren F1, the designers came up with a novel idea. Instead of sitting to one side as in a normal car, the driver sits in the middle, with passengers sitting behind and to either side (below).

DRIVER'S AND PASSENGERS' SEATS

ON THE ROAD

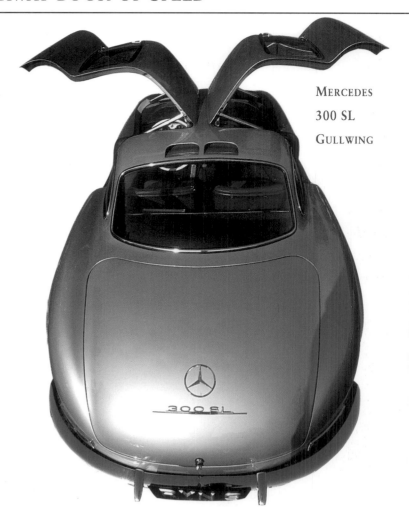

MERCEDES 300 SL GULLWING

The period immediately before and after World War II is often described as the golden age for sporting road cars, such as the Auburn Speedster and the Jaguar XK 120. The Delahaye Type 135 (left) was introduced in the late 1930s. Racing versions of this car had instant successes. Powered by a 3.5-litre (214-cubic in) engine, they won the Le Mans 24-hour race in 1938 as well as the Monte Carlo Rally twice, in 1937 and 1939.

DELAHAYE TYPE 135

JAGUAR E-TYPE FIXED-HEAD COUPE

The Jaguar series 1 E-type fixed-head coupe (below) is as fast as it looks. It has a top speed of 241 km/h (150 mph) and an acceleration of 0–96 km/h (0–60 mph) in a little under seven seconds. Its sleek looks and stunning performance made the E-type one of the classic cars of the 1960s and early 1970s. A total of over 72,000 E-types were built between 1961 and 1974.

MERCEDES 300 SL 'GULLWING'

The Mercedes 300 SL 'Gullwing' (above) gets its nickname from its unusual doors which open vertically rather than horizontally. It is derived from the racing car that won the 1952 Le Mans 24-hour race and was in production from 1954 to 1957.

Because of its racing pedigree, the Gullwing has some impressive performance figures. The 3-litre (183-cubic in) engine could accelerate the car from 0–96 km/h (0–60 mph) in just over 8 seconds, and push it to speeds of up to 265 km/h (165 mph).

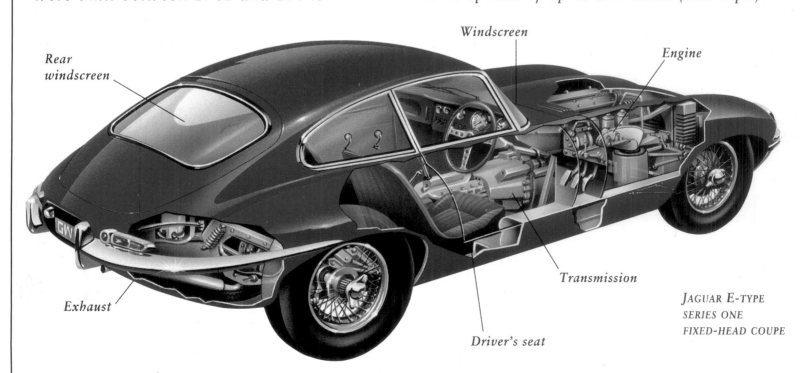

Rear windscreen

Windscreen

Engine

Exhaust

Transmission

Driver's seat

JAGUAR E-TYPE SERIES ONE FIXED-HEAD COUPE

AC COBRA 427

Built between 1965 and 1968, the AC Cobra 427 (right) holds a massive 7-litre (430-cubic in) V-8 Ford Mustang engine. This produces 425 bhp which drives the car to a maximum speed of 265 km/h (165 mph). It can also accelerate from 0–96 km/h (0–60 mph) in a mere 4.2 seconds – in its day it held the record as the car with the world's fastest acceleration!

AC COBRA

FERRARI 275 GTB/4

FERRARI 275 GTB/4

Only 350 of these powerful road cars (left) were built, all between 1966 and 1968. Underneath the bonnet is a 3.3-litre (201-cubic in) V-12 engine that delivers 300 bhp. This means that the car can reach speeds of 257 km/h (160 mph) and accelerate from 0–96 km/h (0–60 mph) in just 5.5 seconds. The 275 paved the way for its successor, the Ferrari Daytona, which was the fastest car of its day with a top speed of 280 km/h (174 mph)!

PORSCHE 356

This car (below) was the 356th project to come from the Porsche design offices (hence the name), yet it was the first car to bear the Porsche name. Like its Porsche-designed predecessor, the Volkswagen Beetle, the 356's engine is in the rear of the car. This 1.6-litre (98-cubic in) engine produces 90 bhp, powering the car to a top speed of 177 km/h (110 mph).

PORSCHE 356

JAGUAR XJ220

The Jaguar XJ220 (below) is truly a 'supercar' – a car whose performance is far superior to normal road cars. Other cars in this class include the Lamborghini Diablo and the McLaren F1 (see pages 4–5). Launched in 1988, the XJ220 boasts a V-6 fuel-injected turbo engine (left) that can accelerate the car from 0–96 km/h (0–60 mph) in an amazing 3.75 seconds. It can also achieve a top speed of 341 km/h (212 mph)!

V-6 JAGUAR ENGINE

JAGUAR XJ220

A PIT STOP DURING THE RACE

FORMULA-ONE RACING is a highly popular sport, drawing huge audiences around the world. These spectators are attracted by the excitement of watching cars hurtle around tracks at high speed. Over the course of sixteen or seventeen races, the racing teams compete for the Driver's and Constructor's Championship. Beyond these races, the teams are constantly improving and testing their cars. All of this is necessary to get the best from driver and machine in a sport where the smallest fraction of a second can be vital.

FORMULA-ONE RACING CAR

PIT STOPS

Pit stops (left) allow cars to maintain their peak performance. Once a car has come to a halt in the pit lane, at least seventeen mechanics work around it, changing tyres, pumping fuel into the tank and even replacing damaged parts. Depending on the amount of work needed, a pit stop can last as little as five seconds.

SAFETY

Safety is paramount in Formula-One racing. The drivers are strapped firmly into a very strong

RACE MARSHALLS EXAMINE A CRASHED CAR

cockpit. In a crash, this remains intact while other parts of the car, such as the wheels, absorb the impact. The car is also fitted with a black box recorder, similar to those found in aircraft. Drivers are also covered in layers of fire-proof clothing.

The track itself is surrounded by crash barriers and walls of tyres. Fire marshalls are also stationed around the circuit and can reach a crashed vehicle within seconds of an incident (above).

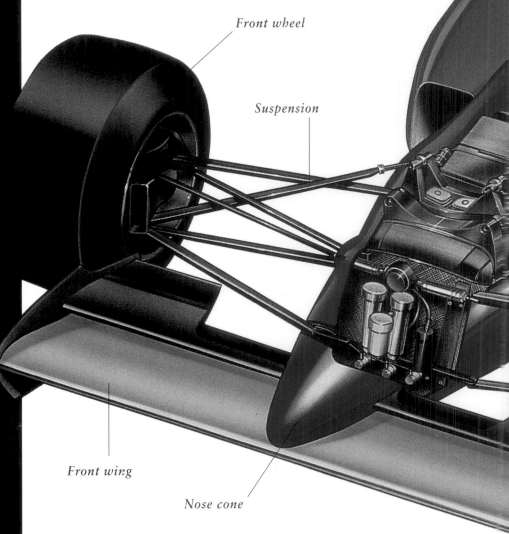

Front wheel

Suspension

Front wing

Nose cone

TYRES

Two types of tyre tread are available for racing. Tyres with a minimum of five treads are used in dry weather conditions and tyres covered in deep treads are

TYRES IN THE WET

used in the wet (above). The latter disperse 26 litres (45 pints) of water from the road surface every second.

FORMULA-ONE RACING CAR

Air intake

Rear wing

Rear wheel

Rear brake disc

V-10 engine

Radiator

Roll bar

Safety harness

Brake discs

ENGINE POWER

Formula-One cars today are powered by 3-litre (183 cubic-in) engines, with varying cylinder layouts, usually V-10 or V-12. These are supplied to the teams by a few manufacturers, such as Ford, Renault, BMW, Honda, Ferrari and Mercedes. Rules now ban the use of turbos and as a result the engines can only produce 700 bhp – in comparison, a V-6 turbo engine produces 1,200 bhp. However, the cars still reach 340 km/h (213 mph) and can cover 1 km (0.6 miles) from a standing start in just 12 seconds!

RACING CARS

During the early days of motor racing, cars were front-engined machines – very different from the sleek cars that race today. The Sunbeam Tourist, built in 1914, had a front-mounted engine and the driver sat upright. Gradually, car body shapes were altered to produce a more streamlined effect. By the 1950s, drivers sat lower down behind much more powerful engines, in such cars as the Type 158 Alfa Romeo and the Mercedes-Benz W196.

1914 SUNBEAM TOURIST

1950 ALFA ROMEO 158

Over the next decades, engines were moved to the backs of cars, monocoque chassis (where the engine forms part of the chassis as opposed to sitting inside one) were introduced, and wings were added to increase the downforce on the car. All of these features were used in the Matra, driven by British driver Jackie Stewart in 1969. The 1973 McLaren-Ford is an example of how radiators were moved from the fronts of cars to the sides, allowing for a more aerodynamic nose.

1954 MERCEDES W196

1969 MATRA

1973 McLAREN-FORD

DRIVERS

JUAN FANGIO

From 1949 to 1958 – Juan Fangio (left) won 34 Grand Prix and the World Championship five times. One of the most successful drivers of recent times was Ayrton Senna (right). He won 41 Grand Prix and the World Championship three times – in 1988, 1990 and 1991, before he was killed in 1994. In 2003, Michael Schumacher completed, his record breaking, sixth World Championship.

AYRTON SENNA

INNOVATIONS

A constant battle exists between car designers, who want to build cars that go as fast as possible, and the sport's law-makers, who want to keep cars' performances within safe limits. Many innovations have been banned. The Chaparral 2E (above) had large, raised wings that were used to improve its roadholding.

CHAPARRAL 2E

Since 1969, wing size has been limited. Six-wheeled cars, such as the Tyrrel P34 (right), were banned in 1976.

TYRREL P34

INDY CAR

Every year, the Indianapolis 500 is held at the world's oldest racetrack, the 4-km (2.5-mile) long 'Brickyard'. 'Indy' cars (right) have powerful V-8 turbo-charged engines, which produce 800 bhp, pushing the cars to speeds of up to 340 km/h (213 mph). Indy races are often held on oval circuits which have banked corners. To cope with these banked curves, drivers can lift one side of their cars using compressed air.

INDY CAR

BENTLY NAPIER

LE MANS ROLLING START

LE MANS

The Le Mans 24-hour race was first held in 1923. Teams raced to see who could drive the furthest during a night and a day around a 13.5-km (8.6-mile) circuit. In the early days, the race was started by the drivers running across the track to their cars. Today, the cars line up behind a slow moving pace car. When the pace car moves aside, the race begins. This is called a rolling start (above).

MONTE CARLO RALLY

This race was first run in 1911 and has been held every year since, except during the two World Wars and the petrol crisis of 1974. During this unique race, hundreds of rally drivers race to Monte Carlo from starting points in Europe and Africa. Weather conditions always prove a key factor. In the harsh winter of 1965, for example, just 22 cars finished out of the 237 that started.

MONTE CARLO RALLY

FORD GT40

FORD GT40

In 1964, the Ford GT40 (above) was introduced to the Le Mans 24-hour race. The car was powered by a 5-litre (305-cubic in) engine and was capable of 264 km/h (164 mph). It failed in its first two attempts to win before taking first place in 1966. The car then asserted its dominance on the track by winning the race for the next three years.

NASCAR

National Association for Stock Car Auto Racing (NASCAR) is a form of racing popular in America. Stock cars speed around paved oval tracks with banked corners. Crashes are common as cars jostle for position during the race.

NASCAR RACING

BURNING RUBBER

ENGINE POWER

Beneath the bonnet of a Funny-Car dragster sits an extremely powerful 8.2-litre (500-cubic in) supercharged engine. Supplying this is a fuel pump that can deliver about 225 litres (50 gallons) of fuel (either nitromethane or an alcohol and methanol mix) each minute. This means that during a five second run, a dragster will use 65 litres (15 gallons) of fuel!

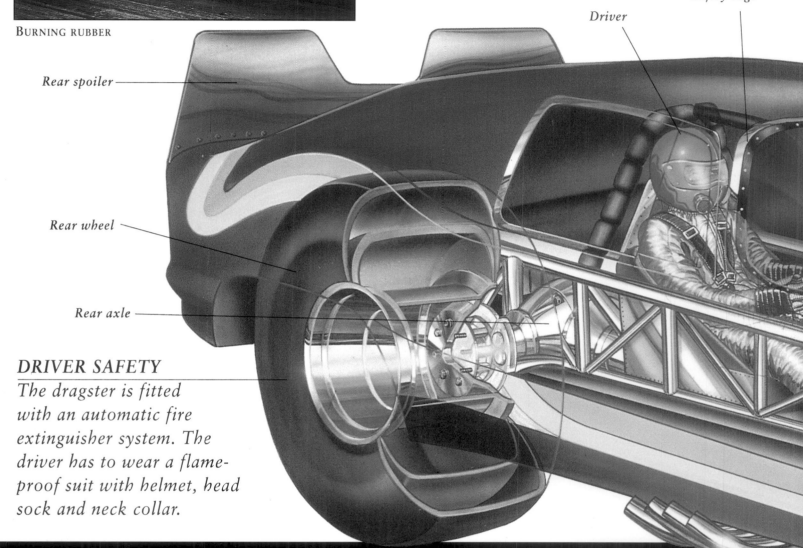

Safety cage

Driver

Rear spoiler

Rear wheel

Rear axle

DRIVER SAFETY

The dragster is fitted with an automatic fire extinguisher system. The driver has to wear a flame-proof suit with helmet, head sock and neck collar.

SINCE ITS EARLY DAYS in the 1930s, Hot Rodding, or Drag Racing as it is now known, has grown into a worldwide sport. During a race, spectacularly fast cars hurtle two at a time down a straight track that is 0.4 km (0.25 miles) long. Today, the fastest of these vehicles can complete the run in a little under five seconds!

So-called Funny Cars (main picture) and their stripped-down cousins, the Top-fuel dragsters (right), use identical engines (see top of page). Funny Cars reach speeds of 465 km/h (290 mph) – slightly slower than Top-Fuel cars. Both kinds of car, though, are fitted with parachutes to help slow them down when they are trying to stop.

FUNNY-CAR
DRAGSTER

*FUNNY-CAR
DRAGSTER*

Engine

SUPERCHARGER

*Sitting on top of the engine is a
supercharger (right). This device is driven
mechanically by the engine and sucks in
an enormous amount of extra air. This
extra air is forced into the cylinders,
where it raises the pressure of the fuel
and air mix. This gives the engine a
massive and immediate surge of power.*

SUPERCHARGED ENGINE

Front wheel

Fuel tank

TOP-FUEL DRAGSTER

LIGHT-WEIGHT BODY

*Funny-Car chassis are surrounded by
bodies made from light-weight carbon
fibre. Overall weight is kept to a
minimum to ensure the fastest-possible
acceleration. In fact, acceleration is
so great that dragsters are fitted with
wheelie bars – long metal bars that
project backwards from the rears to
prevent cars from flipping over.*

GRAND-PRIX RACING BIKE

Windscreen

Kevlar reinforced carbon fibre bodywork

RIDER SAFETY

As with its four-wheeled cousin, motorcycle racing is not without a certain amount of danger (below). To reduce the risk of injury, riders wear hard-wearing leather outfits and crash helmets. Modern crash helmets are made from strong, light glass fibre and plastic. Earlier helmets were made from canvas, cork and leather and only covered the top of the head, giving no protection to the sides.

GRAND PRIX CRASH

KNEE-DOWN CORNERING

Fast corners are usually taken with riders adopting a 'knee-down' position (below). This involves them scraping one of their knees against the track as they lean into the turn. To help them through the corner, riders wear special knee pads covered with hard-wearing solid nylon patches.

Exhaust

Rear wheel

Exhaust

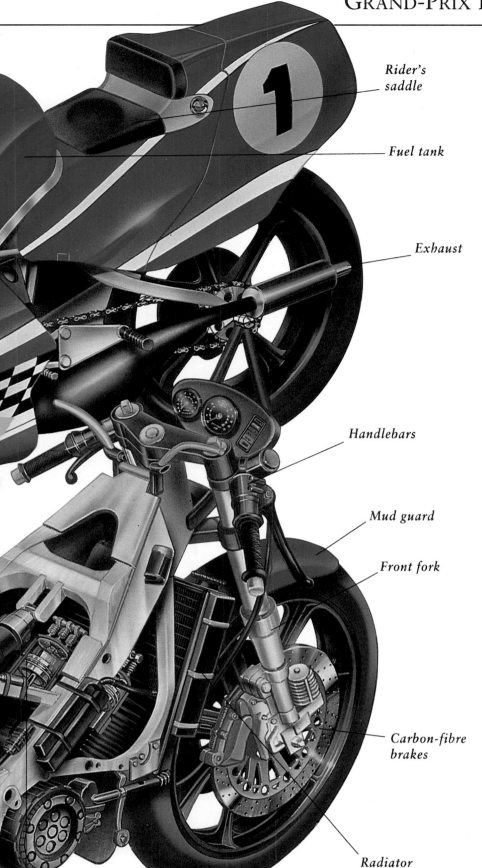

Rider's saddle

Fuel tank

Exhaust

Handlebars

Mud guard

Front fork

Carbon-fibre brakes

Radiator

Front wheel

ENGINE

The engine of a 500-cc (30.5-cubic in) Grand-Prix bike sometimes has four cylinders (right) which hold the pistons. When working at 13,000 rpm, the engine produces up to 170 bhp – more than three times that of the average car to power a vehicle that is only one-fifth the weight.

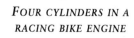

FOUR CYLINDERS IN A RACING BIKE ENGINE

GRAND PRIX START

GRAND-PRIX RACING championships are held in a number of classes, each for different sizes of engine. These range from 125 cc (7.6 cubic in) to 250 cc (15.2 cubic in) and 500 cc (30.5 cubic in). The most powerful Grand-Prix racing bikes can reach nearly 300 km/h (187 mph)!

There is also a Superbike class. Here the bikes have either 750-cc (46-cubic in) four-cylinder engines or 1,000-cc (61-cubic in) two-cylinder engines. However, racing rules state that Superbikes must closely resemble road-going models. As such, their performance is not as good as the Grand-Prix racing bikes – Superbikes can only reach speeds of about 260 km/h (163 mph).

TWO-WHEELED SPEED

The 1920s were a golden age for the world of motorcycling. Companies such as Norton and Indian began to build cheaper and more powerful machines for both racing and normal use. The American ACE motorcycle company made bikes powered by massive four-cylinder engines. In 1923, one of their models, a specially-tuned ACE XP-4 (below) ridden by American, Red Wolverton, established a world motorcycle land-speed record of 210 km/h (130 mph).

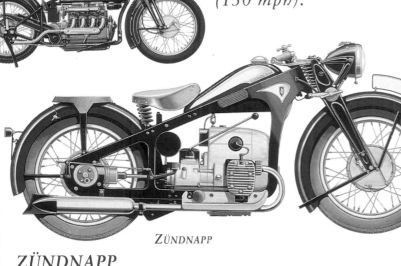

ZÜNDNAPP

ZÜNDNAPP

The 1935 Zündnapp (above) was fitted with a 500-cc (30.5-cubic in) two-cylinder engine. One unusual feature of the bike was the shift stick on one side of the engine. This was used to change gears in the same way as a car. The bike also had a hinged rear mudguard to make it easier to change the rear wheel.

HUSQVARNA V-TWIN

The Swedish Husqvarna company produced 350-cc (21-cubic in) and 500-cc (31.5-cubic in) motorcycles that were successful in road racing during the 1920s and 1930s. The 500-cc (31.5-cubic in) model (below) was capable of 190 km/h (118 mph). Today, the company makes bikes for off-road racing.

MOTORCYCLE LAND-SPEED RECORDS

In the quest for greater speed, motorcycle builders came up with many novel ways to cut through the air. One such attempt was in 1938, when a streamlined body was fitted around a Brough Superior motorcycle. Ridden by British racer E.C. Fernihough, the bike achieved 229 km/h (143 mph) over 1 km (0.6 miles) at the Brooklands racetrack in England – a record for a solo motorcycle. In 1956, a Triumph-powered bike (below) set a record speed of 345 km/h (214 mph) on the Bonneville Salt Flats in Utah, USA. Today's motorcycle land-speed record stands at 519 km/h (323 mph) when Dave Campos of the USA drove his Harley Davidson-powered bike at Bonneville on 14 July 1990.

STREAMLINED BROUGH SUPERIOR

TRIUMPH RECORD BREAKER

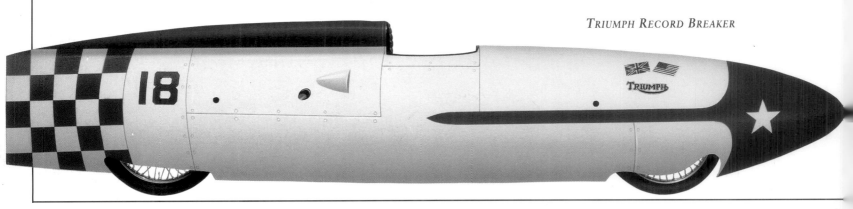

THE NORTON PITS DURING A TT RACE

JAPANESE SUPERBIKES

Today the most powerful road bikes in the world are produced by Japanese companies. The ultimate prize goes to the Honda CBR1100XX Super Blackbird (below). This powerful machine has a 1,137-cc (69-cubic in) four-cylinder engine that can produce 162 bhp. This can accelerate the machine from 0–96 km/h (0–60 mph) in a staggering 2.5 seconds – as fast as a Formula One racing car. The bike has a top speed of 300 km/h (188 mph)!

THE TT RACES

The Isle of Man TT (Tourist Trophy) was first run in 1907. The race snakes its way through the hilly countryside of the island. Early races were dominated by British-built Norton bikes (above and below). Today's TT bikes reach speeds of about 198 km/h (123 mph), completing each lap of the route in a little over 18 minutes.

HONDA CBR1100XX SUPER BLACKBIRD

DRAG BIKES

The fastest drag bikes (below) can cover 0.4 km (0.25 miles) in about 6.5 seconds! During a run these bikes can reach speeds of 328 km/h (205 mph). The engines in these compact machines produce as much power as the fastest production cars, such as the Jaguar XJ220 (see page 7), but the bikes themselves only weigh half as much. The result is an acceleration from 0–96 km/h (0–60 mph) in a little under one second!

NORTON BIKE AT ISLE OF MAN TT RACE

DRAG BIKE

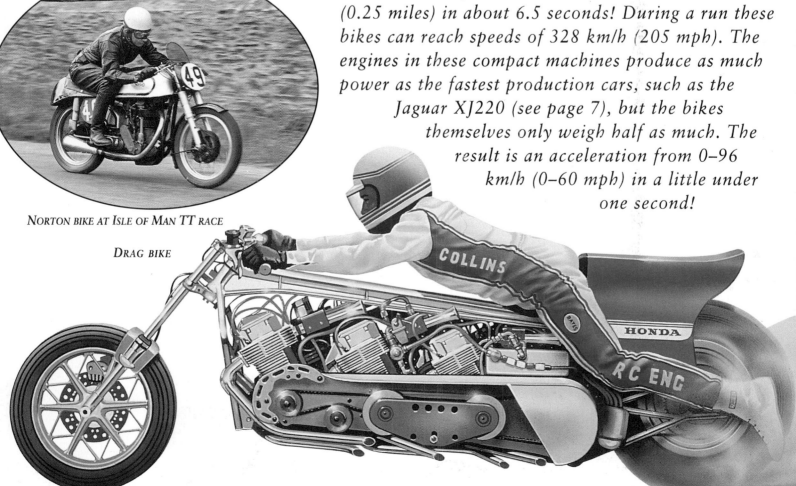

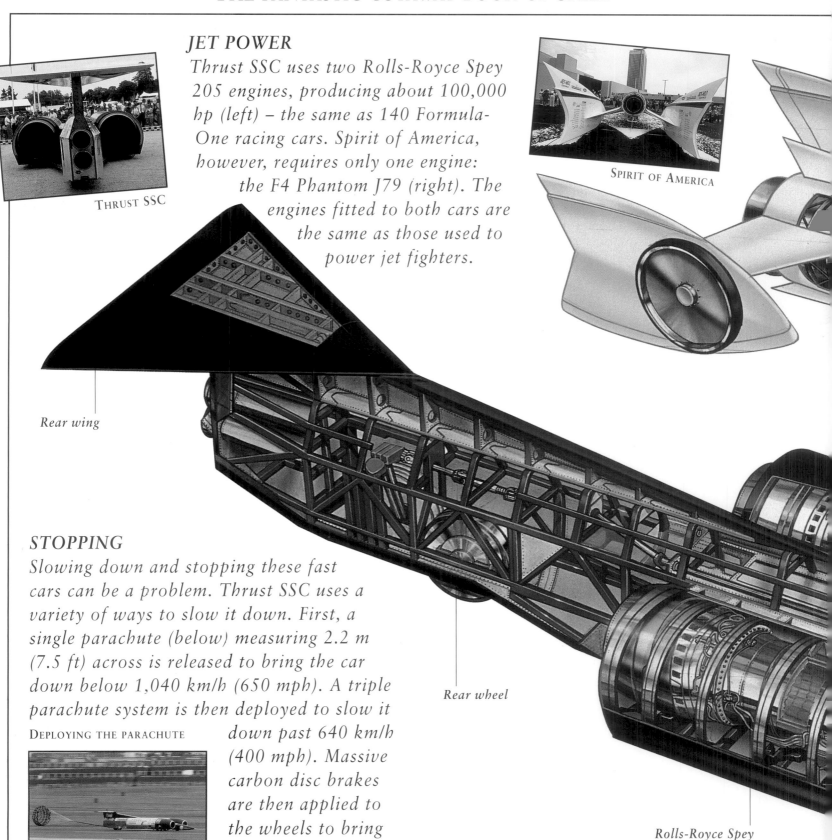

JET POWER

Thrust SSC uses two Rolls-Royce Spey 205 engines, producing about 100,000 hp (left) – the same as 140 Formula-One racing cars. Spirit of America, however, requires only one engine: the F4 Phantom J79 (right). The engines fitted to both cars are the same as those used to power jet fighters.

THRUST SSC

SPIRIT OF AMERICA

Rear wing

STOPPING

Slowing down and stopping these fast cars can be a problem. Thrust SSC uses a variety of ways to slow it down. First, a single parachute (below) measuring 2.2 m (7.5 ft) across is released to bring the car down below 1,040 km/h (650 mph). A triple parachute system is then deployed to slow it down past 640 km/h (400 mph). Massive carbon disc brakes are then applied to the wheels to bring the car to a stop.

DEPLOYING THE PARACHUTE

Rear wheel

Rolls-Royce Spey 205 engines

ALTHOUGH THE SOUND barrier is regularly broken by aircraft, it is far harder for ground-based vehicles to achieve. Thrust SSC set the first supersonic landspeed record of 1228 km/h (763.035 mph) on 15th October 1997 in the Black Rock desert, Nevada, USA. Driven by former British fighter pilot Andrew Green, Thrust SSC acheived the record ahead of the American, Craig Breedlove in his Spirit of America. Both teams had been beset by weather problems and technical difficulties in the chase for the record.

LAND-SPEED ATTEMPT

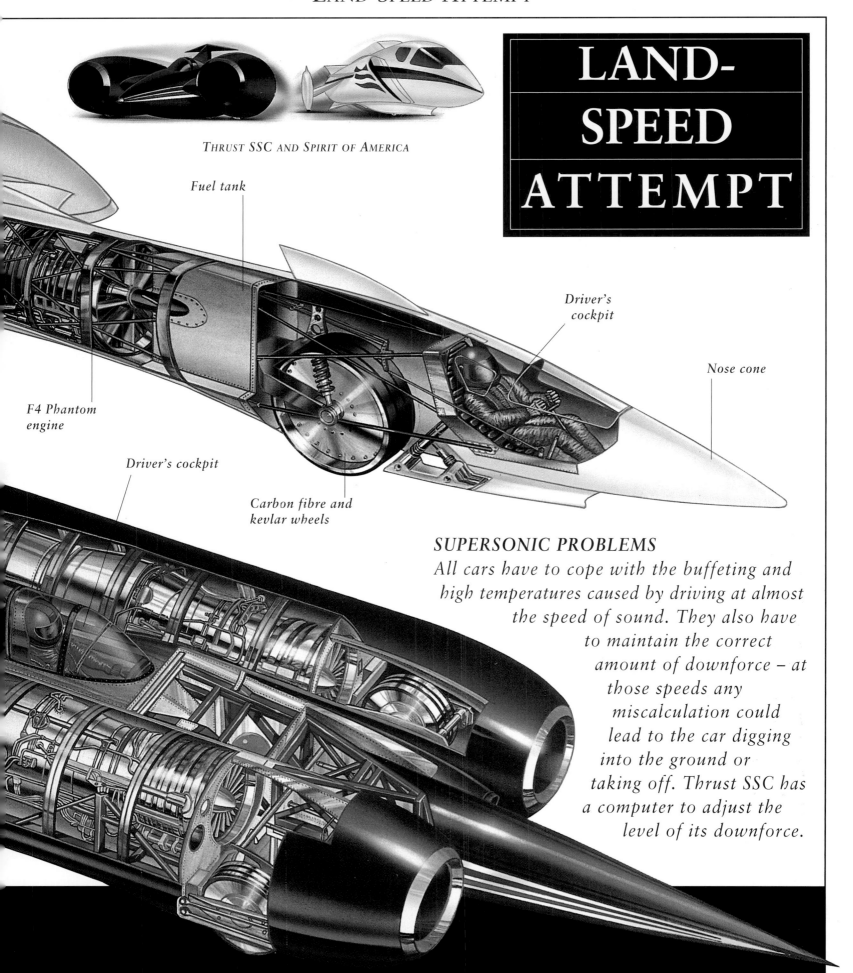

THRUST SSC AND SPIRIT OF AMERICA

Fuel tank

F4 Phantom engine

Driver's cockpit

Carbon fibre and kevlar wheels

Driver's cockpit

Nose cone

SUPERSONIC PROBLEMS
All cars have to cope with the buffeting and high temperatures caused by driving at almost the speed of sound. They also have to maintain the correct amount of downforce – at those speeds any miscalculation could lead to the car digging into the ground or taking off. Thrust SSC has a computer to adjust the level of its downforce.

FACTS AND FIGURES
Both cars differ greatly from each other. Thrust SSC is much larger than its American rival, weighing about 7 tonnes – before its crash Spirit of America weighed only 4.5 tonnes. The American car was 14 m (47 ft) long and nearly 3 m (10 ft) wide, but it is now being rebuilt. Thrust SSC measures over 16 m (54 ft) long and 3.5 m (12 ft) wide.

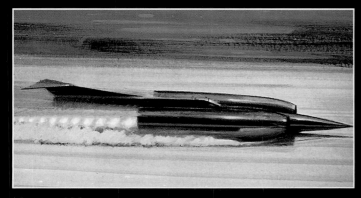

THRUST SSC IN ACTION

FORMER RECORD HOLDERS

RESURRECTED CAR

John Parry Thomas steered his Higham Special called 'Babs' (below) to a record speed of 272 km/h (170 mph) in April 1926. A year later he tried to regain the record that had since been broken by Sir Malcolm Campbell (see below). Sadly, Babs crashed on this attempt, killing the driver. As a mark of respect, the car was buried. Fifty years later, Babs was 'resurrected', restored and is now a museum piece.

JENATZY'S ELECTRIC CAR

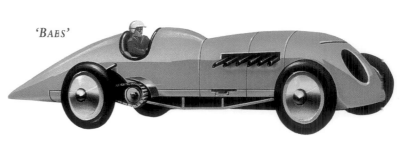

'BABS'

The quest for the land-speed record has led to the creation of some unique cars. The first record holders were either electric- or steam-powered vehicles. One of these electric cars, driven by Frenchman Camille Jenatzy (above), broke the record in 1899, reaching 105 km/h (66 mph). However, it wasn't long before petrol-driven cars asserted their supremacy. The Ford 999 (below) was fitted with a 1.6-litre (100-cubic in) petrol engine. In 1904, Henry Ford himself drove the car across the frozen ice of Lake St.Clair to a record-breaking speed of 147 km/h (91 mph).

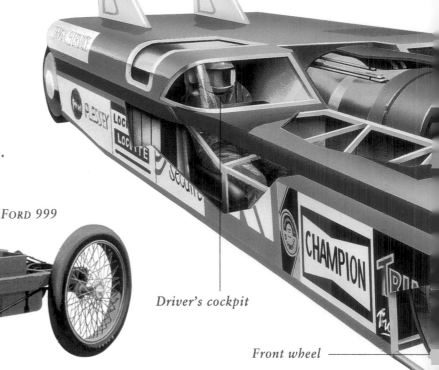

Rear fin

Driver's cockpit

Front wheel

FORD 999

SPEED KINGS

One of the greatest drivers during the years between the wars was Sir Malcolm Campbell who held the land-speed record no less than nine times – he also held the water-speed record! All the cars (and boats) he drove were called Bluebird. One car, driven in 1933 (right), took the record to 436.8 km/h (273 mph). His son Donald continued his father's tradition of calling his vehicles Bluebird. In 1964, his car (below), powered by a Proteus gas turbine engine, set a new land-speed record of 649 km/h (403 mph).

1964 BLUEBIRD

1933 BLUEBIRD

THUNDERBOLT AND RAILTON

Two drivers, George Eyston and John Cobb, dominated the world of land-speed records during the years before and after World War II. Driving the Thunderbolt, an enormous car powered by two Rolls-Royce engines, Eyston pushed the record to 572 km/h (357.5 mph) in 1939. Cobb had to wait eight years before mounting another attempt. His Napier Railton (left) broke the record, reaching 631 km/h (394 mph).

NAPIER RAILTON

SPIRIT OF AMERICA

One of the great speed record drivers of the last thirty years is Craig Breedlove. He has broken the record several times driving some unusual cars. His first success was in 1964, when he steered Spirit of America-Sonic I (right), a three-wheeled jet powered car, to 847 km/h (526 mph). A year later he pushed the record to 966 km/h (601 mph). His latest attempt, in a car also called Spirit of America, is to break the speed of sound (see pages 18-19).

Rolls-Royce
Avon 302 engine

THRUST 2

SPIRIT OF
AMERICA-
SONIC 1

THRUST 2

On 4 October 1983, Richard Noble set a new land-speed record driving Thrust 2 (left) in the Black Rock Desert, Nevada, USA. The car was built around a Rolls-Royce Avon 302 jet engine used in RAF fighter aircraft. Producing 7,700 kg (16,000 lb) of thrust, it powered the car to 1,019 km/h (633 mph). Had it gone 10 km/h (6 mph) faster, the car would have generated enough lift to take off – with disastrous results!

Air intake

THE BLUE
FLAME

THE BLUE FLAME

In 1970, Gary Gabelich steered this rocket-powered car (right) at a speed of 1,016 km/h (631 mph), breaking Craig Breedlove's previous land-speed record (see above). Even though this record was then broken by Thrust 2, the Blue Flame is still the fastest rocket car.

SPEED ON THE WATER

A s trading routes stretched to the very corners of the Earth, a need arose for fast boats to carry cargoes as quickly as possible. Clippers (left) were fast, slender sailing vessels that were developed in the mid-1800s. The name comes from the way the ships appeared to 'clip' the miles off their journey. Clippers could travel nearly 750 km (470 miles) in 24 hours and could cross the Atlantic in as little as 12 days. One of the most famous clippers was the Cutty Sark, which now sits in dry dock in Greenwich, London.

CLIPPER UNDER FULL SAIL

TURBINIA

At the presentation of the British navy to Queen Victoria during her Diamond Jubilee year of 1897, a small boat appeared from nowhere and raced among the battleships. The boat was Turbinia (above), designed by the British engineer Sir Charles Parsons. It was fitted with three steam turbines, each turning a propeller. These drove the boat to a speed of 63.8 km/h (34.5 knots), which was unusually fast for the turn of the century.

WATER WINGS

When travelling at low speeds, a hydrofoil looks just like a normal boat. However, as its speed increases, the boat lifts out of the water, exposing a set of wings underneath the hull. The hydrofoil's wings work by creating less pressure above the wing than underneath (below), pushing the wing up and the boat with it. Because less of the boat is in contact with the water, so friction along the whole hull is reduced, and the hydrofoil can travel at speeds much greater than a normal boat. Typical hydrofoils can travel at speeds of up to 102 km/h (55 knots), but experimental craft have reached speeds of more than 148 km/h (80 knots)!

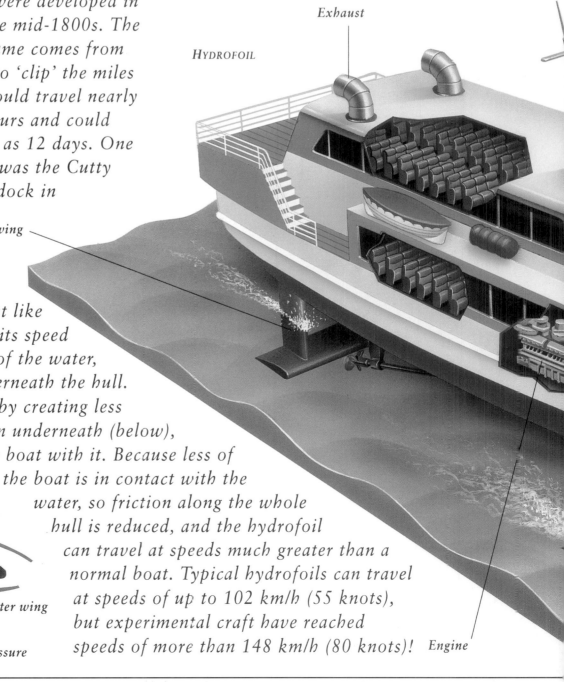

Exhaust

HYDROFOIL

Rear wing

Water flows faster – less pressure

Water wing

Water flows slower – more pressure

Engine

WATER-SPEED RECORDS

The water-speed record has been keenly contested over the years. In 1918, a hydrofoil designed by Alexander Graham Bell set a record of 114 km/h (61.6 knots). Today's official record was set by Kenneth Warby in 1978 and stands at 511 km/h (276 knots). He steered his hydroplane, Spirit of Australia (right), across Blowering Dam Lake in Australia. The boat is also said to have achieved 555 km/h (300 knots), but this could not be confirmed.

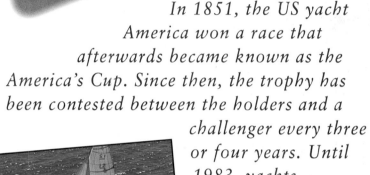

DONALD CAMPBELL AND THE FATAL CRASH IN BLUEBIRD

BLUEBIRD

Following in his father's footsteps (see page 20), Donald Campbell set records on both land and water. In 1964 he set a water speed record of 442 km/h (239 knots) in his boat Bluebird. Three years later he tried to break the 300-knot barrier. However, disaster struck when his boat crashed (above).

AMERICA'S CUP

In 1851, the US yacht America won a race that afterwards became known as the America's Cup. Since then, the trophy has been contested between the holders and a challenger every three or four years. Until 1983, yachts representing the United States won every time. In that year, the yacht Australia 2 took the trophy by winning the series four races to three.

AMERICA'S CUP YACHTS

BLUE RIBAND

The Blue Riband, also called the Hales Trophy, is awarded to the fastest regular commercial crossing of the Atlantic. The current holder is the liner United States which, on its 4-day maiden voyage in July 1952, averaged a speed of 66 km/h (35 knots). It sailed from the Ambrose Light Vessel off America to Bishop Rock lighthouse off Britain in 3 days, 10 hours and 40 minutes.

Front wing

THE LINER UNITED STATES

SINGLE-HULLED POWERBOAT

OFFSHORE POWERBOAT racers are the speed-kings of the water world. The boats they use range from single-hulled vessels with V-shaped bottoms (above) to twin-hulled catamarans (main picture). These powerful boats plough through the open sea, around courses that may be over 400 km (250 miles) long.

Races are between boats of the same engine size, which range in power from 100 to 5,000 hp. The result is a speed of 220 km/h (120 knots) for the more powerful boats!

CUSHION OF AIR

As a twin-hulled powerboat accelerates, air gets trapped in the tunnel between the two hulls and is compressed. This lifts the boat, reducing the amount of the vessel that is in contact with the water, so reducing friction and increasing the speed that the boat can travel.

RACING HYDROPLANES

A similar effect occurs in hydroplanes (above). However, these smaller craft hardly touch the water. Instead, they skim, or 'plane', across the water's surface on a cushion of trapped air.

TWIN-HULLED POWERBOAT

Aluminium hull

TAKING THE KNOCKS

Powerboat racing is a tough sport for both boats and crews. This 15-m (50-ft) long catamaran is strong enough to crash its way through waves that can be 8 m (25 ft) high. To cope with this battering, the hulls are made from hard-wearing aluminium.

INSIDE THE COCKPIT

The driver and the crew member sit one behind the other in a high-tech cockpit resembling that of a fighter jet. In some of the more powerful catamarans, this cockpit can be ejected clear of the boat should an accident occur.

The driver at the front keeps the boat on the right course using electronic navigation systems while the other crew member controls the throttle, adjusting the engine to get the correct speed. Each wears a 'kill-switch', which is a cord attached to the boat which stops the boat if the crew are thrown clear.

THE POWER-BOAT

Rear wing

Throttle controller

Driver

Propeller

Exhaust

Fuel tank

POWERBOAT ENGINES

This catamaran has two 8.2-litre (500-cubic in) V-12 Lamborghini engines positioned in each of its hulls. These powerful engines can accelerate the boat from 0–160 km/h (0–85 knots) in under four seconds. To achieve this, the propellers are sent spinning at up to 10,000 rpm, each throwing up a plume of water, or 'roostertail', that is 30 m (110 ft) long.

GAS GUZZLERS

The two hulls of the catamaran hold the enormous fuel tanks. The engines need a lot of fuel – during a race they can get through about 180 litres (40 gallons) every hour. Fuel is pumped between the two tanks to ensure that the boat stays perfectly balanced.

POWERBOAT IN ACTION

INTO THE SKY

GB SPORTSTER R-1

*I*n the quest for air supremacy, World War I saw the development of faster aircraft than ever before. The Spad 13 (below) was powered by an Hispano-Suiza V-8 engine which pushed it to 210 km/h (130 mph), making it one of the fastest planes of the conflict.

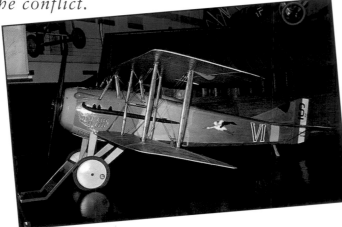

SPAD 13

SUPERMARINE S6B

The French arms manufacturer Jacques Schneider began an annual competition in 1913 to encourage the development of marine aviation – planes that took off and landed on water with the use of floats. Anyone who won the competition three times in a row would win the Schneider Trophy outright – as did the British company Supermarine in 1931. In its final victory, the company entered the S6B (left and right), which flew at 548 km/h (340 mph). The information gained by making the S6B led to the creation of the Spitfire fighter aircraft of World War II.

SUPERMARINE S6B

GB SPORTSTER

The period between the two World Wars saw an increasing interest in flying, especially in races. The GB Sportster R-1 (above) was one of the most successful racing planes of its day. It won the Thompson Trophy Race in 1932 and set a new air-speed record of 477 km/h (296 mph). The tiny plane consisted of a small body fitted behind a huge engine. The R-1's career ended in 1933 when it flipped upside down and crashed during a race.

SUPERMARINE S6B

BACHEM BA.349 NATTER

The German Bachem Ba.349 Natter (right) was designed for use against allied bombers at the end of World War II. Launched vertically, the Natter would soar into the air, reaching a height of 7,500 m (25,000 ft) in only one minute! When in range, the pilot would fire off a battery of rockets. Once done, he ejected and the plane broke in half. The front part would ram anything ahead while the rear would parachute to earth to be reused. Fortunately, it was never used during the war.

Battery of rockets

Pilot's cockpit

BACHEM BA.349 NATTER

Fuel tank

Rocket engine

MESSERSCHMITT ME262

Main fuel tank

Nose cannon

Junkers 'Jumo' engine

Bomb payload

Main undercarriage

Nose undercarriage

BIRTH OF THE JET AIRCRAFT

The idea for a jet-powered aircraft was first patented by English engineer Sir Frank Whittle in the 1930s. However, it was not until the arrival of the German Messerschmitt Me262 (above) in 1944 that jet aircraft were used in World War II. It could fly at 866 km/h (538 mph) and its overall performance was superior to allied jets that came soon after, such as the Gloster Meteor (below). Despite this, the Me262 was built too late and in too few numbers to alter the course of the war.

P-51 MUSTANG

GLOSTER METEOR

NORTH AMERICAN P-51 MUSTANG

The Mustang (above) was fitted with a Rolls-Royce Merlin engine that could push it to 784 km/h (487 mph) making it one of the fastest propeller-driven aircraft of World War II. The ease with which it could be flown earned it the nickname 'the Cadillac of the skies'.

SPEED IN THE AIR

CONVAIR B-58 HUSTLER

SUPERSONIC FIRSTS

In 1953, when it first flew, the North American F-100 Super Sabre (main picture) brought combat aircraft into the supersonic age. This single-seater fighter could reach 1,390 km/h (864 mph), or Mach 1.31. The Convair B-58 Hustler (above) first flew in 1956. It was the first bomber to go beyond Mach 1 and also the first to reach Mach 2. Its maximum speed was 2,215 km/h (1,385 mph), or Mach 2.1.

TU-95/142 'BEAR'

Today's skies are filled with incredibly fast aircraft. Since the end of World War II, the majority of these planes have been jet-powered, sometimes travelling at speeds far beyond the sound barrier. However, many airlines still use propeller aircraft for short flights, while armed forces still have transport and reconnaissance planes, such as the Russian Tu-95/142 'Bear' (above). It is capable of flying at 925 km/h (575 mph), or Mach 0.82, making it the fastest propeller-driven aircraft.

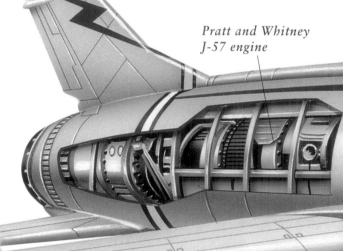

Pratt and Whitney J-57 engine

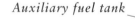

Auxiliary fuel tank

CONCORDE AND CONCORDSKI

The first two supersonic passenger aircraft, the Anglo-French Concorde and the Russian Tupolev Tu-144 (below), appeared in the 1960s. Both aircraft flew at more than twice the speed of sound.

TORNADO

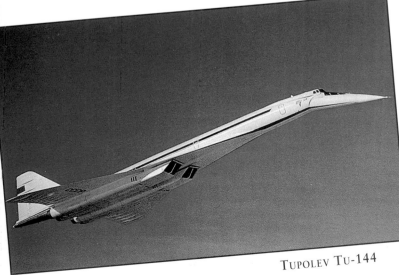

TUPOLEV TU-144

SWINGING WINGS

Several planes use swinging wings to aid their performance, sweeping them forward for slow flight and back for fast flight (right). These include the F-111 and the Tornado (above). The latter can sweep its wings back from 23° to 67° and some versions can fly at 2,414 km/h (1,500 mph), or Mach 2.27.

BLACKBIRD

The Lockheed SR-71 'Blackbird' (right) is the fastest jet-powered aircraft in the world. Powered by two Pratt and Whitney turbo-ramjet engines, the aircraft is capable of reaching 3,530 km/h (2,193 mph) or Mach 3.35. It can fly to the very edge of the atmosphere – a height of 30,000 m (100,000 ft)! Today, several Blackbirds have been given to NASA. They are being used for research into the next generation of supersonic aircraft (see pages 36-37).

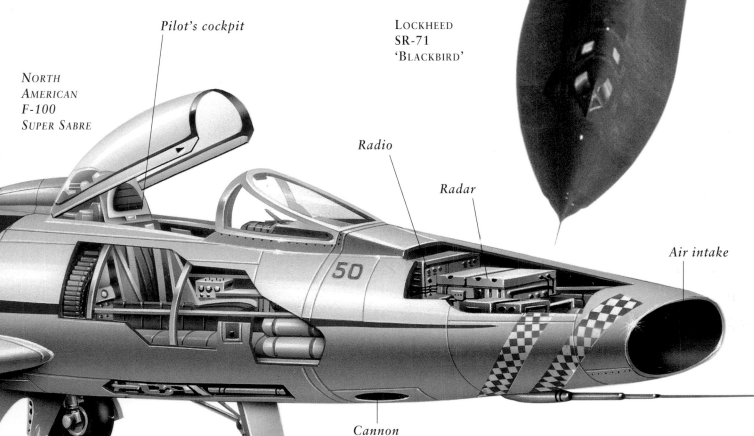

LOCKHEED
SR-71
'BLACKBIRD'

Pilot's cockpit

NORTH
AMERICAN
F-100
SUPER SABRE

Radio

Radar

Air intake

50

Cannon

Nose undercarriage

JETS OF THE FUTURE

EUROFIGHTER

Aircraft designers are always looking for ways to increase aircraft speed or manoeuvrability. This has led to the development of some unique aircraft, such as the Eurofighter (above) and the American YF-22 (left), the experimental version of the F-22 Lightning 2. The Eurofighter has small movable wings, or 'canards'. These allow it to perform manoeuvres that normal aircraft would find impossible. The YF-22 uses 'thrust vectoring' to help steer it. This system involves movable flaps over the exhausts. These flaps deflect the thrust, steering the plane through unconventional manoeuvres. The plane can fly at 2,335 km/h (1,460 mph), or Mach 2.2.

YF-22 IN FLIGHT

THE MIG-31 FOXHOUND

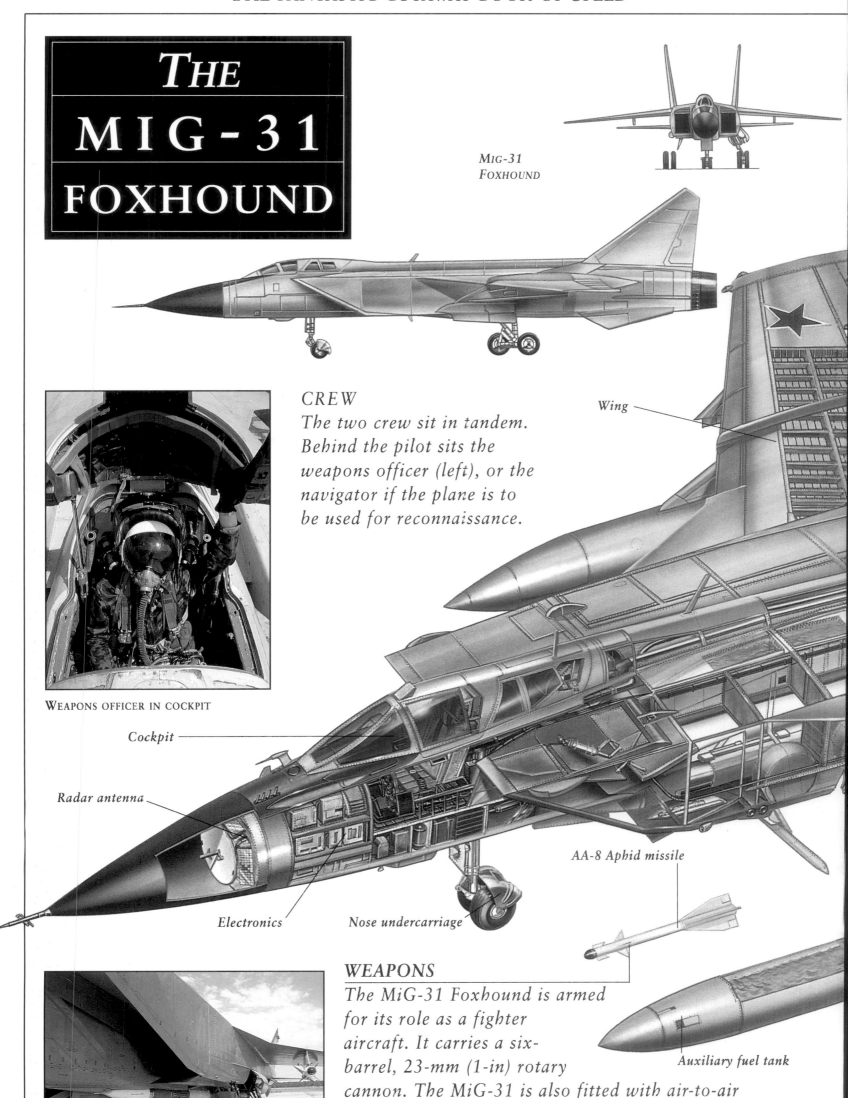

MiG-31
Foxhound

CREW
The two crew sit in tandem.
Behind the pilot sits the
weapons officer (left), or the
navigator if the plane is to
be used for reconnaissance.

Wing

WEAPONS OFFICER IN COCKPIT

Cockpit

Radar antenna

Electronics

Nose undercarriage

AA-8 Aphid missile

Auxiliary fuel tank

MIG-31 CARRYING MISSILES

WEAPONS
The MiG-31 Foxhound is armed
for its role as a fighter
aircraft. It carries a six-
barrel, 23-mm (1-in) rotary
cannon. The MiG-31 is also fitted with air-to-air
missiles (left and above) strapped under its wings.
These include the AA-8 Aphid and the AA-9 Amos
missiles. They allow the Foxhound to engage enemy
aircraft located by radar from a great distance!

POWER PLANT

The MiG-31 Foxhound is powered by two Perm D-30F6 afterburning turbofans. Air for these is sucked through two air intakes and blasted out through twin exhausts creating the massive thrust needed to push it to its maximum speed.

Jet nozzle

Tail fin

MiG-31 DEPLOYING BRAKING PARACHUTE

CAPABLE OF FLYING at a staggering 3,000 km/h (1,875 mph), or Mach 2.83, the MiG-31 Foxhound is the fastest jet fighter in the world. The aircraft was specially designed to fly at great speed at altitudes of up to 20,600 m (67,600 ft). From this great height, it can engage an enemy aircraft quickly and at distance without the need to operate in close combat (see left).

Alternatively, with all of its weapons removed the Foxhound can act as a super-fast reconnaissance plane, flying quickly over enemy positions and monitoring them.

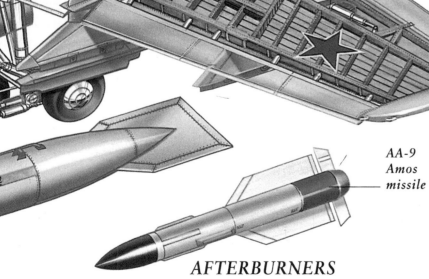

AA-9 Amos missile

AFTERBURNERS

An afterburner is situated between the turbine and the exhaust nozzle of a jet engine. When gases leave the turbine they are still rich in oxygen. The afterburner injects more fuel into these gases and ignites them, raising the temperature greatly. These hotter gases accelerate through the nozzle, increasing the amount of thrust for short periods.

THE X-PLANES

CHUCK YEAGER

After World War II, the newly formed NACA (which later became NASA) started a programme of experimental planes – called X-planes – to extend the performance of aircraft in general. The first X-plane, the Bell X-1 (below), was flown by Chuck Yeager (left) on 14 October 1947 at a speed of 1,078 km/h (670 mph), becoming the first aircraft to fly faster than the speed of sound.

BELL X-1

DOUGLAS X-3

DOUGLAS X-3

The X-3 (left) was a single-seat jet aircraft with a slim body and a tapered nose. During its flying career, between 1952 and 1955, it was used to test the suitability of its dagger-like shape at speeds around the sound barrier.

BELL X-5

Flown between 1951 and 1954, the X-5 (below) was the first aircraft that could reposition its wings while it was in flight. The wings could be swept back to 60°, which allowed better performances at higher speeds, particularly around the speed of sound. The X-5 led to the development of aircraft such as the Tornado and the F-111 (see page 28).

BELL X-5

MARTIN X-24A

The X-24A (below) was part of a project looking into 'lifting bodies' – aircraft that use their fuselage to provide lift and so do not need wings. The X-24A flew at speeds of up to 1,696 km/h (1,060 mph), or Mach 1.6, reaching an altitude of 21,765 m (71,825 ft).

MARTIN X-24B

The X-24B (below), a development of the X-24A, reached 1,865 km/h (1,166 mph), or Mach 1.76, and a height of 29,500 m (97,350 ft). It made its final powered flight in September 1975. Information gained by the lifting bodies, such as the X-24A and X-24B, helped to build the Space Shuttle.

MARTIN X-24A

MARTIN X-24B

ROCKWELL X-31

The X-31 (right) was developed to examine how thrust vectoring and movable canards (see page 29) can be combined to create highly manoeuvrable aircraft. As a result, the X-31 can outrun enemy planes in unusual ways, such as by flying horizontally with its nose pointed up at an angle of 70° – a manoeuvre conventional aircraft would find impossible. It flies at speeds of up to 1,357 km/h (848 mph), or Mach 1.28, and to an altitude of 12,200 m (40,000 ft).

ROCKWELL X-31

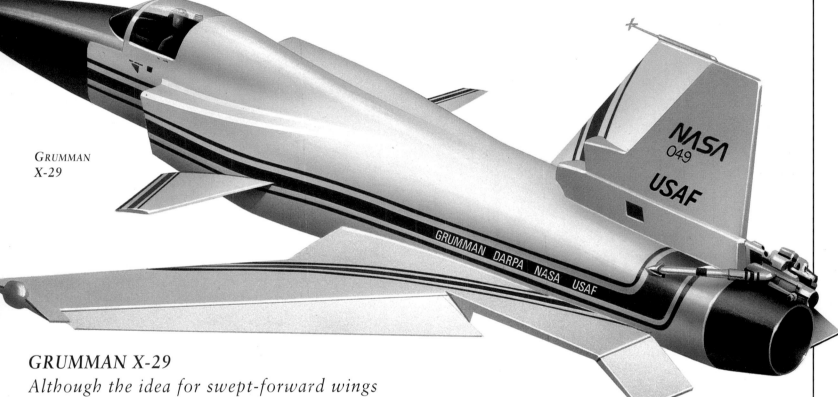

GRUMMAN X-29

GRUMMAN X-29

Although the idea for swept-forward wings is not new (it was first thought up during World War II, but the technology was lacking to build one), the Grumman X-29 (above) is still a revolutionary aircraft. It first flew in December 1984, and since then achieved a maximum speed of 1,696 km/h (1,060 mph), or Mach 1.6, and reached an altitude of 15,150 m (50,000 ft).

The design of the wings makes the X-29 highly manoeuvrable. However, it also makes the aircraft unstable – so much so that the responses of a human pilot would not be quick enough to control it. To overcome this, advanced computers continuously monitor the aircraft and stop it from going out of control.

X-36 and X-45

The unorthodox-looking X-36 (below) lacks a tailplane and is steered by thrust vectoring and movable canards (see page 29). The one quarter-scale model was successfully flown by remote control, using pilots safely on the ground in virtual-reality cockpits. The X-45 is a prototype that will lead to the development of unmanned attack aircraft for the US Air Force.

X-36

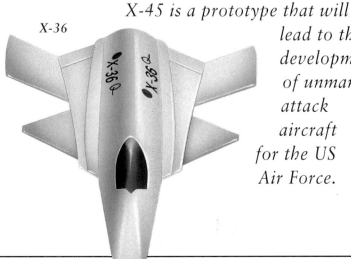

X-15 UNDER THE WING OF A B-52

FIRST FLOWN IN 1959, the X-15 proved an invaluable research aircraft for NASA in its development of the reusable space shuttle. Rather than waste precious fuel on take-off under its own power, the X-15 was launched in the air from a flying B-52 bomber (above). After its launch, the aircraft would climb rapidly to test the effects of flight at heights of up to 107 km (67 miles) above the Earth's surface – some X-15 pilots qualified for astronauts' wings!

Alternatively, the X-15 could burn extra fuel in order to reach astonishing speeds – up to 7,297 km/h (4,534 mph), or Mach 6.7!

AIRCRAFT DIMENSIONS

The X-15 measured 16 m (53 ft) from nose to tail and had a wingspan of 6.7 m (22 ft). It was shaped like a missile with a wedge-shaped tail and thin, stubby wings. When launched, it weighed on average about 15,500 kg (34,000 lbs), depending on the mission. Over half of this weight was made up by the liquid oxygen and anhydrous ammonia propellant needed to fuel the rocket – turning the aircraft into a virtual flying fuel tank!

EJECTOR SEAT

The X-15's ejector seat (left) was designed to save the pilot at supersonic speeds. Rockets would blast the pilot clear, before several parachutes slowed the descent and ensured a safe landing. Fortunately, it was never needed.

FLIGHT CONTROLS

Within the atmosphere, the X-15 was controlled conventionally using flaps and rudders on the wings and tailplane. However, above 36,000 m (120,000 ft) the air is too thin to allow adequate control – the plane was virtually flying through space. As such, the plane had eight small thrust rockets, with which the pilot could control the position of the aircraft as it flew through the upper atmosphere.

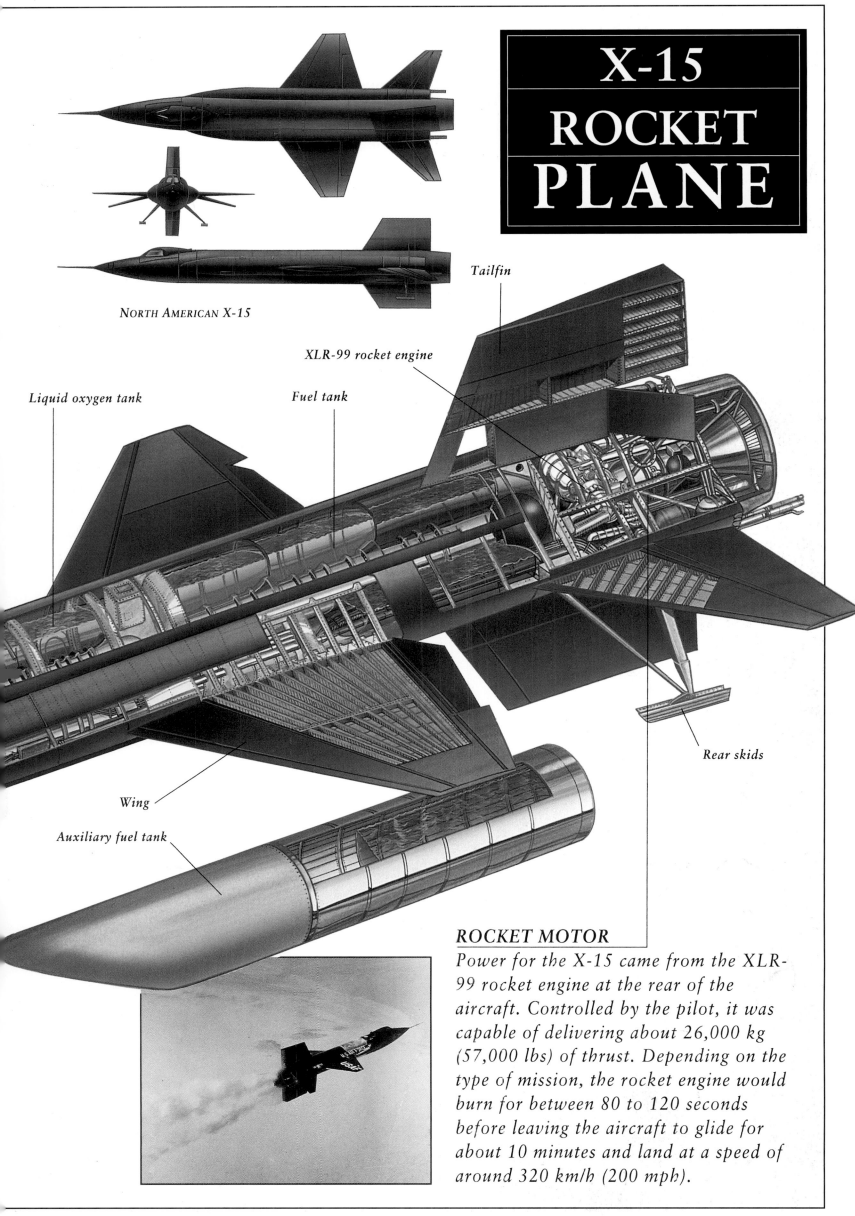

NORTH AMERICAN X-15

X-15 ROCKET PLANE

Tailfin

XLR-99 rocket engine

Fuel tank

Liquid oxygen tank

Rear skids

Wing

Auxiliary fuel tank

ROCKET MOTOR

Power for the X-15 came from the XLR-99 rocket engine at the rear of the aircraft. Controlled by the pilot, it was capable of delivering about 26,000 kg (57,000 lbs) of thrust. Depending on the type of mission, the rocket engine would burn for between 80 to 120 seconds before leaving the aircraft to glide for about 10 minutes and land at a speed of around 320 km/h (200 mph).

THE NASP

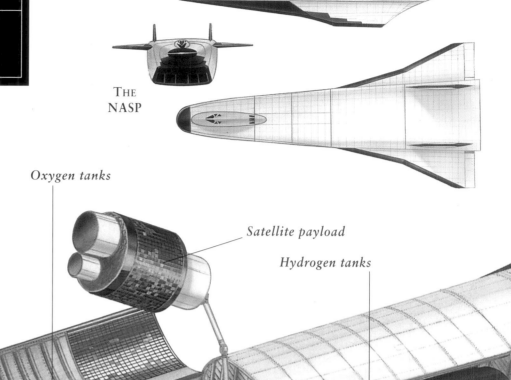

THE NASP

HIGH FLIER

The proposed National Aero-Space Plane (NASP) would be able to carry passengers and satellites at incredible speeds in the upper atmosphere at an altitude of 76.3 km (47.4 miles). The temperature at this height is as much as 1,800°C (3,272°F). To avoid overheating, the very cold 'slush' hydrogen used as fuel (see right) would be stored next to the aircraft's surfaces, forming an insulating barrier against the heat.

Oxygen tanks

Satellite payload

Hydrogen tanks

Nose undercarriage

Cockpit

FUSELAGE AND FUEL

At very high altitudes a normal air-breathing engine would be useless – there is not enough oxygen to keep the fuel burning. The NASP, however, will carry its own supply of oxygen in liquid form along with hydrogen as fuel.

In 2003, the only exsisting supersonic transport aircraft, Concorde, was retired from service after more than thirty years. Today, there are no obvious replacements being developed. Studies are being carried out for the proposed 'children of Concorde', which will have speeds in excess of Mach 2 and will be able to carry up to 300 people halfway around the world without refuelling.

Another suggestion being studied is for a plane that could fly into the upper atmosphere. At these heights frictional forces are lower

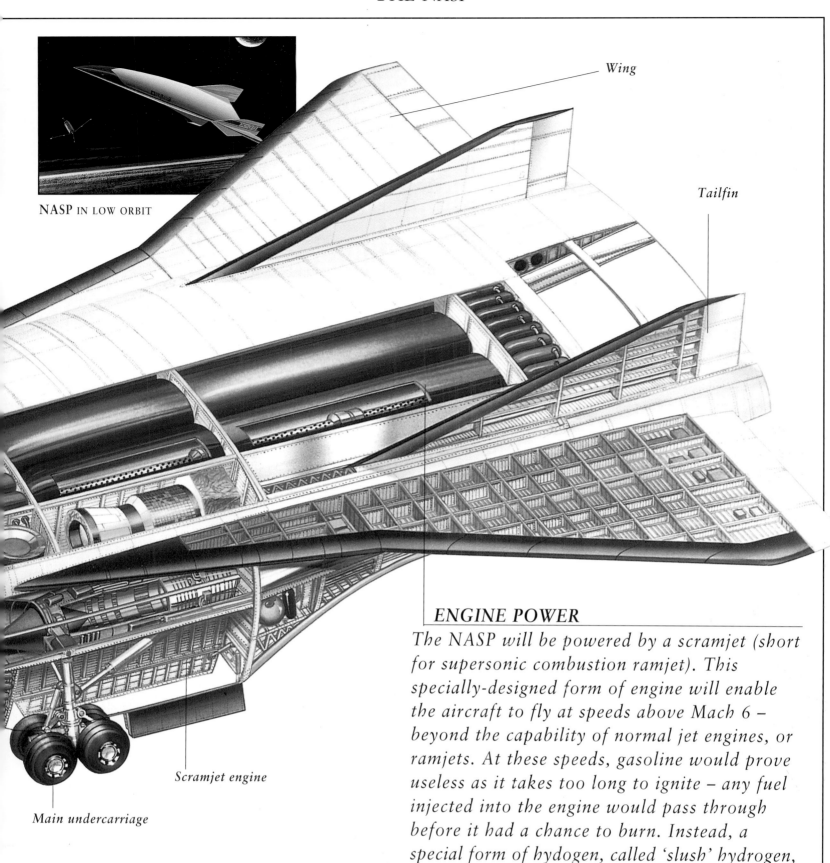

NASP IN LOW ORBIT

Wing

Tailfin

Scramjet engine

Main undercarriage

ENGINE POWER

The NASP will be powered by a scramjet (short for supersonic combustion ramjet). This specially-designed form of engine will enable the aircraft to fly at speeds above Mach 6 – beyond the capability of normal jet engines, or ramjets. At these speeds, gasoline would prove useless as it takes too long to ignite – any fuel injected into the engine would pass through before it had a chance to burn. Instead, a special form of hydogen, called 'slush' hydrogen, which burns much faster, will be used.

because there is very little air. This would let the aircraft fly faster than at lower altitudes. Once in the upper atmosphere, a plane could in theory reach speeds of up to 26,500 km/h (16,560 mph), or Mach 25! Flying this fast would allow us to go around the world in only a couple of hours.

PROPOSED SUCCESSOR TO CONCORDE

GLOSSARY

Aerodynamics
The science of airflow; in particular, how easily vehicles move through air or water.

Afterburner
The device found in some jet engines that injects extra fuel into the engine and re-ignites the exhaust gases to produce a massive increase in thrust.

Altitude
The height above the Earth's surface.

Chassis
Supporting framework for the inner parts of a vehicle such as a car.

Cylinder
A hollow chamber found in engines in which a piston slides up and down.

Downforce
The aerodynamically-produced downward force on a car that improves roadholding.

Engine
The machine that turns energy into force or motion. An internal-combustion engine, such as a petrol or diesel engine, converts energy generated inside its cylinders into motion.

Knot
The unit used to measure a boat's speed, equivalent to one nautical mile per hour – a nautical mile is equivalent to 1.853 km (1.152 miles).

Lift
The upward force that acts on the undersurface of wings as they pass through air or water. This force raises planes into the air and hydrofoil boats out of the water.

Mach number
A number given to speeds in relation to the speed of sound. Hence, a plane flying at Mach 2 is flying at twice the speed of sound. Speeds above Mach 1 are called supersonic.

Piston
A disc or cylinder that moves up and down within a hollow cylinder to drive a vehicle. Pistons can be moved by steam pressure, as in a steam engine, or by pressure from hot gases resulting from the combustion of fuels, as in an internal-combustion engine.

Propellant
An explosive substance that is burned in a rocket or a jet engine to produce thrust.

Propeller
A device with several angled blades that rotates to propel a ship or an aircraft.

Shock absorber
A device that absorbs shocks to the suspension of vehicles.

Speed of sound
The speed at which sound travels through the air. It varies with altitude, so at 12,000 m (39,600 ft) it is 1,060 km/h (662.5 mph), while at ground level it is 1,200 km/h (750 mph).

Supercharger
A device which blows air into the engine inlet to boost its power. It contains a fan driven directly by the engine.

Thrust
The force generated by a jet or rocket engine that pushes a vehicle forward.

Turbine
A motor containing a shaft fitted with blades that is turned by a liquid or a gas .

Turbocharger
A device containing a fan connected to a turbine that is turned by exhaust gases from an engine. It blows air into the cylinders to boost power.

CHRONOLOGY

1897 Turbinia makes its unexpected appearance during a review of the Royal Navy by Queen Victoria.

1899 Camille Jenatzy sets a new land-speed record driving his steam-powered car to 105 km/h (66 mph).

1904 Henry Ford sets a new land-speed record of 147 km/h (91 mph) driving a Ford 999.

1906 First Grand Prix held in France. It was won by Ferenc Szisz driving a Renault.

1907 First Isle of Man TT races held.

1911 January First Monte Carlo rally held. It was won by Rougier, who drove from Paris in a Turcat-Méry.

May First Indianapolis '500' held. It was won by R. Harroun and C. Patscke in a Marmon.

1923 First 24-hour race held at Le Mans. It was won by A. Lagache and R. Leonard, driving a Chenard-Walcker.

1927 John Parry Thomas is killed trying to regain the land-speed record.

1931 The Supermarine S6B wins the Schneider Trophy, flying at a speed of 548 km/h (340 mph).

1935 Sir Malcolm Campbell sets the last of his land-speed records. He drives Bluebird to a top speed of 485 km/h (301 mph).

1944 The Messerschmitt Me262, one of the first jet-powered aircraft, enters service in the German air force, the Luftwaffe.

1947 Chuck Yeager becomes the first man to break the sound barrier, flying the Bell X-1 to a top speed of 1,078 km/h (670 mph).

1950 The first Formula-One car race is held at Silverstone racing circuit.

1952 The liner United States wins the Blue Riband for setting the fastest commercial crossing of the Atlantic. It averaged a speed of 66 km/h (35 knots).

1964 July Donald Campbell sets a new land-speed record of 649 km/h (403 mph) in the gas turbine-driven Bluebird.

October Craig Breedlove sets the first of his land-speed records, pushing the top speed to 754 km/h (469 mph) in the three-wheeled Spirit of America.

1966 W.J. Knight pilots the North American X-15 to a speed of 7,297 km/h (4,534 mph), or Mach 6.7.

1967 Donald Campbell is killed trying to set a new water-speed record.

1969 Concorde becomes the first supersonic airliner to enter service. It flew at speeds of up to 2,333 km/h (1,450 mph), or Mach 2.2.

1970 The rocket-powered Blue Flame sets a new land-speed record when it reaches 1,002 km/h (622 mph) driven by Gary Gabelich. This is still a record for a rocket-powered car.

1976 Captain Eldon Joersz and Major George Morgan set a new air-speed record for a jet aircraft of 3,530 km/h (2,193 mph), or Mach 3.35, flying a Lockheed SR-71 Blackbird.

1978 Kenneth Warby sets a new water-speed record of 511 km/h (276 knots) in the Spirit of Australia.

1983 Richard Noble steers the jet-powered Thrust 2 to a new land-speed record of 1,019 km/h (633 mph).

1985 Robert Barber breaks the 79-year-old record for a steam-powered car. His vehicle Steamin' Demon reaches 234 km/h (146 mph).

1990 Dave Campos sets a new motorcycle-speed record of 519 km/h (323 mph).

1997 The British former fighter pilot Andrew Green sets the first supersonic land-speed record in the Thrust SSC reaching 1,288 km/h (765.035 mph)

2003 Concorde touches down after its last ever commercial flight.

INDEX

Photographic credits:

Abbreviations: t-top, m-middle, b-bottom, r-right, l-left

Pages 4, 5 both, 7tl & br, 10 both, 11ml & mr, 12, 13b, 14m,
15, 18tl & tr, 19b, 23m, 24 both, 25, 27bl, 28br, 29 all & 32 t –
Rex Features. 6t, 7tr, m & bl, 8 both, 9, 11tl & tr, 13t, 14b, 18b,
30 both & 31 – Frank Spooner Pictures. 11b – British Film
Institute.16m, 17t & b, 22tl, 23t & inset, 23b & 27br –
Hulton Getty Collection. 17m – Honda UK. 22tr –
Mary Evans Picture Library. 26 both, 28tl, tr & bl,
32ml , mr & b, 32, 34tr 35b & 37t – The
Aviation Picture Library. 34tl –
Rockwell Aerospace. 37b –
British Aerospace.